Who Can I Talk To?

Talking It Out

Dwayne Booker

SOCIAL AND EMOTIONAL LEARNING FOR THE REAL WORLD™

Rosen Classroom™

What do you do when you're sad?
What do you do when you're mad?

Dealing with feelings can be hard. You have many tools you can use.

You can breathe deeply.
You can go for a walk.
You can talk it out!

Talking it out is very helpful.
Who can you talk to?

You can talk to a trusted adult.
They will listen to you.

Talk to your parents.
They can give you ideas
about how to act.

Talk to your teacher.
They can help you find the right tools to solve a problem.

Talk to your coach.
They can help you do your best.

Talk to a friend.
They can help you feel better.
They might know how it feels!

You are not alone.
You can talk it out!

Words to Know

coach

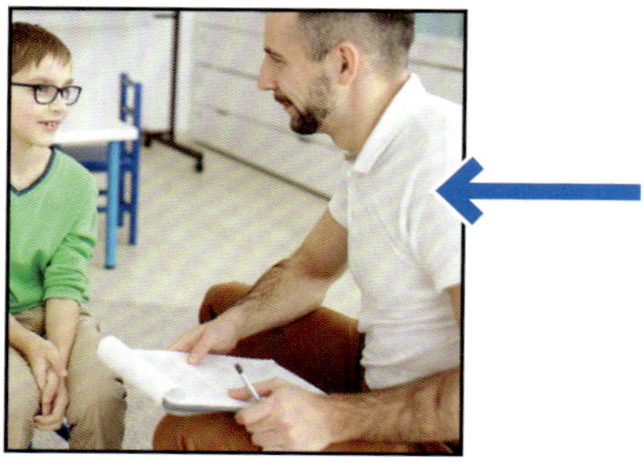

teacher